Butterfli

Eyes

love poems, quotes, and notes

Shynae Nicole

Written by Shynae Nicole
Cover Design by Brently Pearson & Phillip Johnson
Copyright 2016 by Shynae N. Davis
All Rights Reserved.

Books may be purchased in quantity by contacting the publisher at My Mind In Ink, PO Box 3642, Mount Vernon, NY 10553 or the author at www.shynaenicole.com or by email at shynae@ShynaeNicole.com.

Please note the definitions at the beginning of each chapter were taken from the online Merriam-Webster Dictionary. They are not my personal definitions or words.

This book is dedicated to all the lost ones, hopeless romantics, and soul searchers. May we never give up in finding our way. May we love like we've never been hurt. Still believe like doubt is not second nature. May we always experience life with the tenacity to prosper.

TABLE OF CONTENTS

LOVE   11

DOUBT   33

LIFE   57

Acknowledgments

Poetry has been the single most important and constant outlet in my life. Writing poetry allows me to relive important events and rewrite undesired endings. The poet, Anaïs Nin, stated, "We write to taste life twice, in the moment and in retrospect." I am certain there are millions of reasons why people write poetry, memoirs, short stories, and/or novels. The common thread is that all writers have a story to tell, whether fiction or non-fiction. Poetry has allowed me to tame my wild overactive imagination and channel it on paper to develop a storyline. My poetry is a journey of experiencing life through love and doubt.

To all the boys I've loved before...You have given me the greatest and most self-defining moments. At times I thought I could not love. While other times it amazed me how much love I could give. From the breakups I learned all good things must come to an end. From perseverance I was taught all bad things also must come to an end.

Mariel, Brently, Aja, and Jesus H.T. thank you for being a part of this process.

To my friends and family, the support and encouragement you give is unparalleled.

Mom, I am forever indebted to you. You show me daily what love does and does not look like.

Bonjour

I feel compelled to tell you
How I feel
Everything
My unbiased truths
Honesty described on blank canvases
Perfectly defined by lines
Ready to be filled
With emotions
Cries and laughter
Story-telling of desperate attempts
The unfolding story of me
While I allow you to explore
The depths of my despair
So let's begin...

Permeable Membrane

"I disappear into the person I love.
I am the permeable membrane.
If I love you...
You can have it all.
My money, my time, my body
my dog's money.
I will assume your debts and project upon you all sorts of nifty
qualities. You never actually cultivated in yourself.
I will give you all this and more.
Until I am so exhausted and depleted and the only way I can recover
is by becoming infatuated with someone else."

-Elizabeth Gilbert
A monologue from the movie Eat, Pray, Love

love

noun \ ˈləv

a feeling of strong or constant affection for a person

attraction that includes sexual desire : the strong affection felt by people who have a romantic relationship

a person you love in a romantic way

Sometimes there's no good explanation to why you love, like, or want someone to be a part of your life. More times than not searching for superficial reasons to satisfy others' curiosities only take away from your raw emotions. To justify your emotions, you come up with all kinds of equivocal answers. Because really you can't quite put your finger on why you feel so deeply about a person. They're the first person you think of every day. You pray for them more than you pray for yourself at night. It's as simple as the way your heart beats when you see them. It's how after years you still want to look your best for them. It's sweaty palms and butterflies. How you wake up just a few minutes before them to catch the sun graze off their face. It's how the future never seemed brighter and the past was so bland without them. Sometimes there are too many reasons and sometimes there are not enough. Whatever the reason may be, you shouldn't be questioned about why you *love*. If they have to ask undoubtedly they've never felt anything equivalent. Therefore, no justification you give them will satisfy their-inquisitions.

and I loved you like I had never been hurt before. it was my mistake,
I loved you too raw.

Deadly Sin

When it comes to you
I'm a glutton for punishment
What hurts most
Is how easily you give things to others
Things I've struggled so hard with
Yet still never received.

In the three years since we've met
Nothing has changed
I'm an adult
Therefore,
I recognize I put myself in this predicament
I know I've stayed willingly
And for as long as I have
I cannot help the way I feel about you
Which causes me to constantly
Keep in contact with you
Perpetuating this toxic cycle.

What's evident is
You've moved on
Desperately,
I want to do the same
I no longer want to be angry
Or hate you
Although,
I am upset about what has transpired
Or maybe
I'm more disappointed
About what hasn't happened.

I want to get to a place where
I'm emotionally disconnected from you
A place I can be objective
I know that won't be tomorrow
But with time hopefully
I will get there.

Depth

It is him I should be with
He who loves me more
But mediocre love is not one
I desire
I yearn for a love
I can drown in
Suffocate
Lose myself
Then find myself all over again

Niche

When it's "the one"
You just know it
Because things that used to be difficult
Are now simple.
What was once hard
Is easy.
Like trusting, loving, sharing, caring, changing,
Opening up your heart, and making things work.
Being completely comfortable in your own skin.
Turning flaws into beauty marks.
Handling obstacles with the confidence to triumphant.
Together anything is possible
Divided we fall.
Putting respect before love
Death before dishonor.
Loving unconditionally
Knowing something is wrong
Before anything is said.
Motivating and being motivated
To do more, be more, want more.
Being challenged to do all things previously desired
But hindered by fear.
FINALLY achieving that satisfying feeling
That is attained by knowing this is
ABSOLUTELY the person God put on this earth
Just. For. You.
Created perfectly for each other.
Apart just merely two individuals struggling.
Together you make an unbreakable bond
That can survive
ANYTHING.
I MEAN ANYTHING, ANYTHING.
Because you LOVE, RESPECT, and TRUST each other.
With those three things who wouldn't be able to prevail?

Tough Talk

It's crazy, how I actually contemplated giving it all up for him. Three years of hard work could have all come crumbling down. As he whispered in my ear, telling me everything I wanted to hear. Quickly, I forgot about the independent mantra I recited after my ex left. Just so I could fall peacefully in his arms and feel the warmth of his lips on mine as we kissed.

There was a part of me that desperately wanted to pull myself away from him. So I could distance myself and recollect my thoughts. Then the other half of me only wanted to get closer. So close until we were officially connected as one. As we discreetly moaned each other's names. No matter how many times I told myself "this is always how it is in the beginning". My heart didn't seem to understand.

Slowly but surely I lost my composure. After too many "I miss you" and "I can't wait to see you" text messages permeated my night vision. I ended all my goodnight texts with a kissy face. I would have given it all up for him. Just another kiss could have justified my actions. When we kissed we made love with our tongues. No one existed until we came up for air. Then the world disappeared as we went for more.

Then one day immediately after goodnight I was about to say "I love you". I stopped believing in Fairy Tales a long time ago. Shortly after, I discarded the idea of happy endings and Prince Charming. So who could he have possibly been?

Even though he never found my glass slipper and didn't rescue me from a tall building because my hair wasn't that long. I will always remember how he made me feel. He made me happy. That may be far from a happy ending but for me it was close enough.

Just Give Up

I thought he surrendered
He continues to test me.
Making me run through
Crack pipe alleyways
With bruised knuckles.
He continues to test me.
Thinking that he is so opaque
I can't see through him.
Every time he picks up the phone
It leaves an impression on his skin.
When he goes to see her
I can sniff her scent.
I can see the lipstick that was once there.
But wiped away by fear
Too afraid I would notice that was not
The shade of red I wear.

When will he surrender?
He is so transparent
Everything he has done in the dark
Has come to light.
Tell me why has he not surrendered yet?
He is like an army with two men
Still fighting for victory
But only doomed for defeat.
Tell me why has he not surrendered yet?
Given up that crazy life
Made me his wife?

I stand in a puddle of blood
With black and blue hands.
From trying to find him on foreign land.
Knocking on various doors
Desperately searching for him.
He didn't come home last night.
I know he's out there
Somewhere.

Sitting in a car is far too overrated
I choose to raid places.
Flipping beds.
Trashing closets.
Snatching down shower curtains.
I want to see his face.
I just can't understand
How I continue to sustain this treatment.

I want him to surrender his heart to me.
Pour out all his love
Give it to me in a diamond encrusted cup.
Beg for me to take it.
I want him to surrender to me.
Give up his former lifestyle.
Settle down.
Become a man.
Say I do.

Gravity

A powerful force
Beyond control
A fire ignited
A flame lit
Completely infatuated
Intoxicated
Poverty-Stricken
Famished
As long as
Love is here
I could sustain
Off pure energy
That's how desperate
I am for you.

Red Matter

There used to be ***this woman***
When she walked heads turned
When she spoke men and women listened
No light was needed
Her smile lit gloomy rooms
Her laugh, it was infectious
Needless to say it was contagious

When she was around
There was no need for dictionaries
She read books for leisure
Knowledge and intelligence
Ran through this woman's veins
Beauty draped this woman
She wore elegance as an accessory
She was not easily angered
Nor was she temperamental
Every action was carefully constructed
Every decision was precisely planned

This woman only had one flaw- she loved
This woman loved Love
But Love did not love this woman
She loved wholeheartedly
She loved naively
She loved foolishly
She loved Love until it became her downfall
In the end, it was what caused her demise

This woman no longer loves
She no longer laughs
Nor does she smile
Beauty drapes this woman uncomfortably
Elegance barely lingers near her presence
She is bitter, angry, and no longer turns heads

She cares about nothing in the world
All she ever says is
"Screw Lover! Love don't live here!"
So no one bothers to listens
Love was her drug
She was never strong enough
To fight her addiction
There used to be *this woman*.

Hypocrites

They keep telling me
hate is a strong word
But so is *love*
That doesn't stop them from
throwing that word around.

Irony

All I ever wanted
Was to be loved.
The sad thing is
Love is often given so freely to the
Undeserving.
Seldom is it granted to the
Earnest.

Without a Hitch

I want to run away with you.
Strut down the longest runway of my life
With my father by my side
Until he hands me off
We stand face to face
Eyes glistening
Eager to say
I do
Love you
And until death
Do we part.

Picturesque

On Sundays we stay in bed
We only get out to
Use the bathroom
Eat
Or make coffee
Your image is imprinted
So deeply in my mind
When we leave on Mondays
I find pieces of you
In every beautiful thing I see.

Heart Stroke

When I speak of
Heartaches & Heartbreaks
I will go back to *that summer.*
The summer...
That was carried away by
Expectations
Possibilities
And Maybes.
The summer...
My emotions led me to
Unreciprocated connections.
In a matter of weeks
Everything changed.
We met.
I fell hard.
He fell off.
The summer...
That hurt so badly
I could barely sleep.
The summer it was hard to eat.
The summer it took 3 years to recoup from.

When I speak of...
Heartaches & Heartbreaks
I will go back to *that summer.*
The summer...
I sold myself short for
Some kind words
And the possibility of a Lover.
The summer...
I was desperate and impatient
So we never waited.
The summer...
I was more infatuated with the idea of love
Than love actually.
The summer...
I was heartbroken by my
Almost Lover.

Dirty Laundry

He was like
Thanksgiving
And Christmas Eve
Savory
And full of surprises.
Fire
And Ice
The way he made me hot
Then meticulously
Cooled me down.
When he'd leave
I'd stay in bed
Sleep all day
In the same stained sheets.

Exploration

When we met
I thought I had found
Everything great in the world
Until you left
I realized
There is so much more
Of the world to be seen
Good-bye.

Don't Be One of Those Needy Women

You are the single most important person in this world to me. You are my best friend. My biggest supporter. My therapist. My life coach. My financial advisor. The list goes on and on. I can only hope that I am half the woman you are. You are self-less, nurturing, patient, and wise.

I respect you even more for being a single parent and never once complaining about it. You became a homeowner just to give me and my sisters a place to call our own. I admire your passion and drive to go back to school and obtain your degree. You are the epitome of strength, integrity, and loyalty.

I have always strived to make you proud. Even as an adult, I never want to let you down. Although, when it comes to matters of the heart I feel as if I often do. I know I haven't lived up to your expectations in that department. Sometimes I sit and wonder how I could come from a woman like you? A woman so strong. A woman so fearless. A woman so tenacious. I feel like your polar opposite. Believe me, I've tried hard to live up to the standards you've set. Time after time I've failed. The fact is I'm just not you. I love differently than you. I love hard. I am emotional, overzealous, and even dramatic at times.

However, your voice is always in the back of my head. "Don't be one of those needy women." "No man wants a doormat." "Stand your ground." Thank you for being the strong independent woman I can always look up to.

Mom,

I love you beyond words.

To My Wonderful Daughter,

I know you think that when it comes to having a relationship I'm hardcore, emotionless, and unaffectionate. Those characteristics don't describe my true emotional-self. I am just like you. I love very hard, but I have learned that there must be a balance in every aspect of life even in love. The fact is nothing in life is free. Therefore, a man who gets the core of my heart must be worthy of it. Not only with words, but with actions as well. He must win me over. I say these things to you because you are worthy of nothing but the best. Your knight will come, and he will prove himself to be worthy of your love. There will be no room for doubt, his sincere love for you will reveal itself. "A dream you dream alone is only a dream. A dream you dream together is reality" John Lennon.

It's a man's job to woo you, don't settle and don't give in to the BS. Keep your most precious prize to yourself until he proves worthy of it. You have a lot more than just sex to offer any man. You are an Ace with great qualities. "To love is nothing. To be loved is something. But to love and be loved, that's everything!" T. Tolis.

Love,

Mom

doubt

verb \ 'daůt

to be uncertain about (something)

to believe that (something) may not be true or is unlikely

to have no confidence in (someone or something)

Some mornings I need a little extra reminding of just how amazing my mind, body, and soul are. This might come naturally to some but I'm honest enough to say, it doesn't for me. There is no shame in learning to love myself in my twenties. I give love to others but seldom to myself. I will grow to love myself and the things I cannot grow to love I will work to change and what I cannot change I will learn to accept.

and the very moment she learned to fly was exactly when
she found a nest to rest in.

Deprivation

The one at the biggest disadvantage
Is the one who has yet to experience great things
For it is that person who takes everything given to him
Like it is gold
Even if it is worthless in value
Void of effort
And lacks consistency.

That person is at a disadvantage
Because he goes through life thinking
the smallest simplest mediocre things are great
So he sees no discrepancies with the little given to him
Until he is given what he truly deserves
It is only then he realizes the deprivation he has long endured.
Know your worth.

Unfair Exchanges

You have my heart
This means you have me
Some years ago I gave it to you
While you spread me apart
Licked my fears away
Penetrated my thoughts
Caressed my hopes
Massaged areas
I would only allow you to reach
As much as I have fought to get it back
Every attempt has been unsuccessful
When I'm too feeble
Too exhausted
Too drained
To spar, to argue, to grapple
I go on a hiatus
Until I've regained my strength
Then the sequence starts over again
Spread
Lick
Penetrate
Caress
Massage
I lose myself every time I seek to gain you
In and out you go with ease
While I barely hold on
Struggling to let go
I forget if I'm fighting for your heart or my own
It seems synonymous at this point
Getting your heart would give me back mine
The hardest part is recovering the Me
I was before you
This unrequited love
Has slowly killed me
Death must be easier than
Living without you
So I let you spread, lick, penetrate, caress, massage me
Since those are the only places we agree.

Queendom Unknown

It must be hard trying to find yourself
In different men trying to find themselves
It is too difficult a task to bare
To gain self-worth
In different men looking to society for
A sense of worthiness
Women are of men
There is no wonder why
You would sacrifice everything for men
For a small piece of identity
Using the apex of your thighs
While you vet
It must be hard trying to find yourself
In different men ignorant to the mere definition of
a woman's worth
Society will never view men how women do
Oh, how hard it is being women
King look to her for she is your-Queen.

Affirmations

I said this every morning until I believed every word:
I am beautiful.
I am smart.
I am the best.
I deserve the best.
My body is perfectly fine. No alterations needed.
I am caring, loving, funny, intelligent.
I am hard-working, dedicated, ambitious, loyal.
I am enough!
My flaws make me who I am. I embrace these differences.
I am the total package; there is no need to settle.
I am worthy of true love.
I love myself just the way I am.
I am enough!
I am enough!
I am not my weight.
I am not my hair.
I am not my complexion.
I am not how much money I make.
I am not the clothes I wear.
I am everything.
I am too much to be listed.
I am too complex to put into words.
But I am enough!

It took me 3 years and 4 months until I believed every word.

Seventeen and Lost

Little Black Girl lost
I'm lost...
In my thoughts, my ideas, my world
Soul searching for a while
Still I know nothing about myself
My future is one I have always wondered about
My only dream was to be daddy's little girl
But he was never around.
It seems my fate is to be
Seventeen and pregnant
Seventeen and crying all night
Seventeen and never seeing my full potential
This baby won't go to sleep
Now look at me
Just another statistic
Another black girl drop out
Staying home with a child.
My mom kicked me out.
My man is nowhere to be found.
He convinced to have his baby
Then he left
Seventeen and lost
With no idea
What real is from reality
Dreams are from illusions
Little Black girl lost
I'm lost...
In my thoughts, my ideas, my world
Screaming inside for some rescuing
Soul searching for a while
Still I know nothing about myself
Seventeen and lost
With no hope
Someone will find me
I'm so lost.
I can't even find myself.

Psychosis

Uncontrollable laughter
Intimacy without ever being touched
Subtle neck kisses
Foot rubs
The smell of coffee brewing in the morning
Midnight confessions
Interlocked fingers
Safe places.

Unwanted tears
Absence welcomed by fear
Sweat and sex in the air
Terms of agreement left uncommitted
Pent up aggressions
Promises unkempt
Unanswered questions
Inabilities
Insecurities
Uncertainties
Driving me wild.

Peace

My skin
No longer feels itchy
I don't stare in the mirror
For hours analyzing every flaw
Wondering why I am not as pretty
As the other girls
The extra pounds
Don't bother me anymore
They actually make me feel sexy
Like a woman in my own right
All the things I once cursed
My wide hips, full lips, overly plump breast
I now embrace
They are Me.

Defiance

Incomplete without it
Never fully complete with it
Love to hate it
And hate to love it
I miss it so much
But happy it's gone

Hopefully the last good-bye
Wasn't the last time
I get to say hello
But if the last hello
Was the first real Good-bye
I'm thankful

Finally strong enough to walk away
But always too weak to stay
So I sway
Gravitating forward and backward
Backward and forward...
Until it's all just a vague memory.

Responsive

Resilient and strong
The way I bend
But never ever do I break
I may scream from the unbearable pain
But never ever do I surrender
Beautiful
No, not my physical being
The beauty of my forgiving heart
The beauty in my teary eyes
But still I choose to see the good
When I place my hand over my chest
It's still there
It still answers to touch
Broken and battered.
Abused and misused.
My heart…
It's still there.
Apprehensive and unsure
But still willing.

Battle

I have always struggled with self-acceptance. Constantly, thinking I should look a certain way, act a certain way, have a certain lifestyle, fit a certain size. I was never truly happy. Even now when someone calls me beautiful, intelligent, or commends me on my accomplishments I have a hard time believing them. I hesitate to respond deeply pondering if those things accurately describe me. If those things could actually be true about me. I harp so much on the negative aspects of my life. Mentally, I never give the positives a chance to flourish.

It is so much easier to see and believe all your flaws and negatives in life. Relentlessly, trying to correct the imperfections. Never fully acknowledging your beauty, growth, strength, and ambition. Every single day I struggle. I force myself to believe that I am beautiful, I am smart, I am loving, I am worthy of great things, and that I am enough. On the days when I feel insufficient, small, and unimportant I remind myself even if I see myself as all those things. The world views me as much more. Ironically others see more potential in me than I sometimes see in myself.

Why

You will always be blind to your potential
If when you look in the mirror
You only seek out reasons for your failures
Instead of reasons why you succeed.

Discomfort Zones

When they look at me,
Quickly I look away.
So they stare,
Mesmerized
And I run and hide
Sinking deep down
Hoping to disappear
I hate it
When they stare
Feeling like they can see
Straight through me
All my insecurities
All my imperfections
All my flaws
Swiftly adding disclaimers
After their compliments
Never- just "Thank You"
I hate I can't see what they see.

Feeble

I haven't mustered up the courage
to delete your pictures out my phone.
So I quickly scroll past them
Ensuring I never catch a glimpse of your face.

Beauti-fly

Who would have ever guessed
You'd be so vibrant
Full of life
Adventurous
Never fearing heights
Who would have ever guessed
You'd be such an iconic symbol
Standing for growth
Transformation
Evolution
You are beautiful
I only wish you were aware of this too.

Muse

When you're not around
I long for you
Thinking of ways we can reconnect
So many things I want to share with you
But I keep it all inside
Fearing I will never find something
That allows me to be exactly who I am
Like you
Handwritten on plain sheets
My outlet
The things I tell you
I could never say to the world
The purest form of me
I place on you.

Her

I wanted to hate her, but I couldn't.
I tried many times to stop watching
But I was hooked.
I wanted to know what happened.
I wanted to see if they worked out.
Or maybe I wanted to see if they didn't.

Fate

Everything happens for a reason
There are no coincidences in the world.
Not the freckle on my face
Nor the twitch in my eye.
What is meant for me, I will receive.
What I do not receive, was never meant for me.
I will compete with no woman.
And wait for no man.
There are no coincidences.
Not the love I lost nor the love I never found.
What is meant to be will be.

Disinterested

I am no longer interested in being amidst
Busy days
Long shifts
Extreme tiredness
Which causes you to be so preoccupied
You either
Forgot
Never bothered
Or didn't care enough
To respond to my "Good Morning" text
Sent at 9:16am
Two days ago
I am no longer interested in being
Your afterthought.

Constellation

I've prayed on the same star for 365 days
Yet I'm still here
If only wishes came true on the first try
If only dreams were fulfilled after awakening.
A constant in an inconsistent world
Big City, Bigger Visions
Aware of the fact what is wanted
Is not always what is received
A thousand wishes were made
None came true
How unfair
Starving artist
Begging for change
Tell me what more do I have to sacrifice
What more does it take to be everything
I know I have the potential to be?

REM

I refuse to believe what we had was a fixation of my imagination.
It felt so real. It can't be fiction because when I woke from the dream
my phalanges smelt of his being. We were walking barefoot holding
hands on the beach. The ocean swallowed our feet. The further we
walked the clearer I could see how truly meant together we were to
be.

Suddenly he disappeared. The only traces of his presence were
indentations in the sand trailing away from me. Fatigued and sore
with lactate muscles. But I had not been to the gym. It was from
constantly pushing myself on to him. He made my palms sweat and
heart race every time my retina captured a snapshot of his beautiful
face.

Oh, how beautiful his face was to me. Everything perfectly and
meticulously placed in the precise spot. His skin was sun-kissed until
his complexion turned to the ideal shade. When he smiled he blinded
me his teeth shined so bright I could never clearly see. Every time we
were together he violated my personal space. It gave me a chance to
inhale his scent until I had enough bottled up to save for a rainy day.

Repeatedly, I went over everything in my head. Every conversation.
Every interaction. Every text message. Desperately, I tried to
decipher all the events. Finally, enough courage was attained to ask
questions. A distant voice was heard. A flicker of light seen. My eyes
flew open. There was an abrupt end. Was it all a figment of my
imagination? An illusion? A delusion due to my yearning heart? It
felt so real.

life

noun \ '*līf*\

the ability to grow, change, etc., that separates plants and animals
from things like water or rocks

the period of time when a person is alive

the experience of being alive

For the majority of my life I've had a void. A void I haven't been able to fill with men, material things, or even money. When I was a child, I wanted to be a teenager. When I was a teenager, I wanted to be an adult. Now I'm an adult and I want to be something else. I've gone my whole life with the notion of being dissatisfied. I was never content and always wanted more. However, adulthood has made me realize happiness comes from within. Every failed relationship whether it be lover or friend has taken a piece of me with them. Over the years, I've lost the confidence in my ability to cultivate and mend. I've waited a lifetime for this one magical thing to happen to me. In my mind this *"one thing"* will change every other aspect in my life. I don't know if I will ever find what I've been "searching" for all these years. However, I've worked very hard on being happy and content with my life and circumstances. I pray every day for the career, love, and family I've long dreamed of. More importantly I pray every day for a peace of mind.

and the worst part is…letting go of what you think you may never
find again.

Entry

Date March 10, 2008
Time 1:01 am
Place the discomfort of my own home
What am I doing is the question I keep asking myself
While tears stream down my cheek
Staring in the mirror at a perfect woman who is so imperfect
I am ruining my life and
The only person I have to blame for my unhappiness is me
I beg for his deliverance
As I plead for his forgiveness
For I have sinned
I count 1 2 3 4 5

Today was the first time
I begged for God to help me love myself
I asked for help to learn my worth
To realize it is not contingent on a man
I want to love away all the insecurities that haunt me
Making me do the most shameful things
My head in the toilet as I binge
I lay on my back as I cringe
Similar to an addict,
That can't help but fall victim to their addiction
I cannot help but make bad decisions.

One is for loving a man more than I loved myself
It runs down my leg as I stand
He has injected me with a healthy specimen of semen
Standing not ashamed
But happy he came, inside me
My ignorance ran deeper than ever imagined
Instead of seeing it as degrading
I felt I had been upgraded
Honorable enough for him to use me as a nest for breeding
While I waited to see if I would ever bleed again.

Two is for loving a man just so he would stay
I did the walk of shame 4 am one day
Tears rolled down my face as I covered the pillow over my face
Disgraced as he pumped away
Too scared to walk out the door when he told me to leave
Upset I told him "no, not tonight"
He said I should go
So I laid down, shut up, and opened up
Right after he was done
I ran out
Halted back to the car
Tears too impatient to wait fell right there.

Three is for being with a man because there was no one else
Embarrassed by face, insulted by taste
I scrubbed away one whole layer of skin trying to erase
What happened at his place
Desperately trying to forget
While I convinced myself everything would be alright
Never wanting to see him again
But that still didn't stop me from being with him
Over and over
Each time in the shower clogging the drain with more layers of skin.

Four is for letting someone in my life who I knew had an
agenda
We laid peacefully and serene as the sun rose
Awakened by his alarm, he got up, and put his clothes on
He left me feeling good for the moment
But worse by the minute
Knowing I could never be of any significance
I had given it up too quickly
He calls and all my fears diminish
But are immediately replenished
When he expressed his distaste for me
Uncertain of how I felt
I cried as I listened to love songs all night.

Five is for caring about a man who was physically and mentally unavailable
It was a rainy day, a couple's kind of night
I didn't want to be known as a home wrecker
But we wrecked his house
I tried to hold my composure, he kissed my neck, and it was over
He lasted for 5 minutes
Thinking about her had him impotent
Feeling worthless, I just got up and left.

I count *1 2 3 4 5*
From today forward
I will love myself
I will love away all the insecurities making me do the most shameful things.
My body shall be my temple
No longer will I lay on beds heavy with the scent of different men.

Empire

Summer nights
How nice
Cool crisp breeze
Just right
Sirens
Horns
Whistles
And Bells
The city that never sleeps
Oh how I love thee.

Alumnae

I'm kind of happy
I'm kind of sad
I want to cry
I want to laugh
When I look into my past
I see no one that resembles me
So I climb up a tall tree
Squint my eyes
But still I can't see
So I turn around
To penetrate my future
Suddenly,
I see a generation of people
That look just like me
People that look up to me
Sometimes I want to give up
Sometimes I want to keep going
Sometimes I wish I wasn't the first
So I wouldn't have to carry all the burden
They depend heavily on me
They watch my every move
And instantly become captivated
If I don't do it for me
I will do it for them
I am the precedent.

Blocked and Bothered

What do I write about
When I am so emotional
I can barely hold the pen
What do I write about
When I feel
So depleted
Broken
Battered
I can't even form a sentence
The words
Just don't make sense
The world
I can't make sense of it
What do I write about
On days like this
When...
My lips won't stop quivering
Eyes won't stop crying
Nose won't stop running
When...
I am so emotional
I can barely hold the pen
What do I write about
When the paper won't stay dry?

Play Bill

Deception when allied with theatricality is a powerful device.
Light however is a weapon against all evil.
Misinterpretations of personal perceptions
Engage audiences as they seek for insight.
Sweat and tears shed on a stage
Big enough to act out dreams.
As they sit and stare
"Oh" and "Ah"
Clap and cry
The final act quickly appears.
As they stand and applaud
Holler and whistle
Begging for encores.
The curtains slowly covers their faces
As they graciously bow.
The absence of light
Left them standing frightened
As the weapon they once used
Was no longer present.
And the deception of the theatrical characters
Left them in awe.

Bon Appetite

As I stroked your neck with my nose
The blood rushed to my upper thighs.
Pulsating.
Sweating.
As you stared into my eyes
I familiarized myself with your smile.
In a room full of people
It felt like it was just us.
As we kissed
Then talked
Consumed our food
Kissed some more
The waitress came
To ask if we wanted dessert
We instantly looked at each other
Knowing what we wanted
Wasn't on the menu to be served.

Diamond

Moans and groans
Bites and licks
Where pleasure meets pain
Flesh on flesh
Until pressure takes over
We release
Then I unleash my hold.

The Color of Life

I have been called everything from negro to colored. But now I am black with a capital "B". Because that's the category that fits my color of skin. So what else will they call me to make me feel like nothing?

They say it is not always about race or black and white faces. But the places you have been and pace you travel to get to new stages. Being that my race held me in one place for too many stages of my life caused me to become complacent in this place that separates black from white faces.

So now I am free. But the damage has already been done. It will be centuries before I get back what was taken. It kills me to know my own family hates me. They take one glance and only see my ebony complexion. If they stared long enough they would see underneath ebony lies ivory. The complexity of my complexion goes far beyond the mind's capacity to see. If they could see for more than just sight and use their sight to see. They would see we share the same family. Somewhere down my family tree hung a bunch of bastard kids. Whose biological fathers had ivory skin. It kills me to know that my own family hates me. I can't change the pigment of my skin or kin.

They say the world is not just black or white but every shade in between. Since white is the absence of color and black is the absence of light. So I ask them if the world is not just black and white, why has it taken until the 21st century to elect a black president? As if the color of a person's skin dictates competence.

It seems no matter how many degrees we acquire somehow we will always be seen as illiterate. Or how many homes we purchase from dedication and hard work we will always be known as hopeless, homeless, and hungry. I just want to be seen equally. So when you look at me do not see me as the *absence of light.*
*B*ut as the ***Color of Life.***

Feverish

Smiling
Wondering what
He or she will look like
Hoping she has my eyes
He has his nose
Curly black hair
Then I stop
Think
10 fingers
10 toes
Everything else will be fine
Impatiently waiting
Until maternal instincts are second nature
Proudly crowned with that title
I'll daydream about them until then.

Candid Conversations

We talk every night.
About everything
Love, life, theater, art.
She is an exceptional listener.
Advice giver.
Very opinionated.
Not easily persuaded.
Always honest.
My consolation, she is.
There is so much comfort
In telling her my unspoken thoughts.
She listens. She smiles. Then speaks.

My daily stories are entertaining to her.
Sometimes...
She does not remember all the characters.
So she asks the same questions twice.
I repeat the beginning.
I repeat the end.
But still I enjoy telling her them.
Like reciting poetry from a book.
She listens intently.

She sees so much potential in me.
Things I vaguely see. She sees vividly.
I sit in awe, as she reads my life's narrative.
Clairvoyance.
Injections of hope and self-confidence
Are administered as we converse.
I give her youth.
In exchange for wisdom, knowledge, and grace.

She could be my great-grandmother.
I could be her child's child.
But somehow we manage to connect deeply.
Strangely we equally empathize.
Our friendship was unexpected, greatly appreciated.
She gave me...inspiration.
I take it everywhere I go.

Let It Go

The beat dropped and my heart sunk
All too familiar with his melancholy words
He sung with such soul and declaration
I believed every word
Without question
Then the chorus came
I too sung along
I sung loud
I sung hard
I sung without pause
Until I actually believed
Everything would be okay
Then the end came
I felt my world had fallen apart
So I quickly played it again
Until the only way I felt unworried
Was to leave it on repeat.

Bounded

Growing up
I always looked up to her
Mimicking how she spoke
Copying the way she dressed
The first person
I ever wanted to be just like
She took care of me
Kept me safe
Over time we became
Disconnected
Similar to strangers
Time heals all wounds
So maybe,
One day
We'll be reunited
Tightly bounded
Like when we were younger.

Thief

You stole her from me
She talked about you all summer
Counting down the days until her departure
Until you two would be together
Even while we roamed Rome
She spoke of you
The daunting feeling of knowing
When we returned
I'd only have her for a few more weeks
Was overwhelming
She tried calming me
Saying she'd come back in a year
But I knew deep down
When she got to you
She'd be too enthralled to return
I lost her just like that
Without a fighting chance
Los Angeles
You stole her from me.

Roulette

Refuse to flinch
Refuse to wince
Give any sign of nervousness
Any sign of weakness
Staring straight into the barrel
Looking right at the screen
Unbothered
Standing firm
Determined not to give in
Not to be the first to…
Call.

Selfish

My mind no longer races to you
When my favorite love song comes on
Happy moments are contently
Unaccompanied by your presence
Never have I felt more beautiful
Than
Without you
I no longer pray it will be you
Standing teary-eyed
At the end of the altar
The one tightly gripping my hand
As I push and scream
Instructing me to breathe
I no longer crave a life with you
Or yearn to wake up next to you
Never have I felt freer
Than
Without you
Never have I been this happy
This at peace
Never have I been so in love with
Me.

No Work Necessary

All his demands were met
Without question
He was given all of her
But seldom did he give any of himself
He liked a certain kind of woman
A woman that was hard to catch
And even harder to keep
So when he was finished
After he got everything he wanted
Without any regard
He discarded her
He just didn't like
Things that came easy.

Simplicity

The things that make me most happy
Are the simple pleasures of life
Cliché quotes.
Soulful melancholy music.
Spoken Word.
Poetry, Mine and others.
A savory glass of wine.
Flowers on the first date.
Rainy days in bed.
Deep conversations with Mom.
Swaying my hips to the beat.
Plies, Pirouettes, Developpes, Arabesques.
Knee deep in the Mediterranean Sea.
Swimming in the Caribbean.
Delicious dessert followed by flavorful food.
I am most happy that the simple pleasures
Are available for me to enjoy.

Jasper

She called me frantically
She loved him
Like no other boy
She loved before.

She brings him up
Every now and then
Wondering how a life
With him
Would have been.

Dressed in all black
She peacefully laid him to rest
Weeping with only her grief
As proof of his existence.

She brings him up
Every now and then
But when she does
She never calls him
By his first name
She just calls him baby.

Garden of Butterflies

In my garden of butterflies
Is where they come to be inspired
They enter naïve and exit with knowledge
In my garden of butterflies
Limitless possibilities lie
Transformation transpires
In my garden of butterflies
They enter debilitated
Exit rejuvenated
Where youth is no longer desired
In my garden of butterflies
Exploration begins after chrysalis ends
They enter young
Exit mature
Arrive scared
Escape secure
In my garden of butterflies
They never grow old
They are vintage essentials equipped with life's tools
In my garden of butterflies
The butterfly is the ultimate sign of beauty
Completion of a transformation
They all must make it through
Child to adult
Caterpillar to butterfly
In my garden of butterflies
Is where *life* hides.

Artistic Expressions

I write best when I am
Either
Losing myself
Or
Finding myself.

Treble & Bass Clefs

My favorite songs
Make me want to cry
More than they
Make me smile
There is beauty in pain
Strength in vulnerability.

Ranting and Raving

I can't contain the fact I'm discontented with this particular aspect of my life. I want butterflies but somehow I seem to always end up with teary eyes. I have a beautiful life, and I don't take it for granted at all. I just feel like *something* is missing. It's disheartening to watch, what seems like, everyone getting married or having children. As I sit and ponder the uncertainties of my future. In the past, I have pushed "good guys" away while clinging to unscrupulous ones. I know, "patience is a virtue." I know, "If it's meant to be it will be." I know, "nothing happens before its time." I know "when you least expect it that's when it will happen." I'm human so I still get impatient. I get lonely. I get nervous at the thought those things may never happen for me.

My friend's response to my rant was everything I needed to hear. "That's life. Embrace it. We live beautiful lives. We love. We are loved. And sometimes that's all that matters. Trust me. God designed this...It always works out. I promise. I think sometimes there's a lesson behind our stories. It's weird. Life seems complete with a partner and children but we all get there at different times or maybe not at all. Appreciate what you have and see how much more blessed you'll be." Thank you for that Toya.

Au Revoir

This is not the end.
It's merely the beginning.
This is not the end.
It's only
The start of my
Entire life.
This is not the end.
But somehow
I feel compelled to say
Good-bye.

Thank you for purchasing Butterflies & Teary Eyes

I'd love to hear from you.
Shynae@ShynaeNicole.com
Or
visit: www.shynaenicole.com

Made in the USA
Middletown, DE
01 July 2016